Ancient Secrets for a Healthy Home

**Environmentally Friendly, Healing, Invigorating
Removing Stagnant Energy**

Mallory Neeve Wilkins

Mallory Neeve Wilkins

Ancient Secrets for a Healthy Home
Environmentally Friendly, Healing, Invigorating
Removing Stagnant Energy

Copyright August 2016 - Mallory Neeve Wilkins

All rights reserved. No part of this publication can be reproduced, stored in a retrieval system or transmitted in any form or by any means – electronic, mechanical, photocopying, and recording or otherwise – without the prior written permission of the author, except for brief passages quoted by a reviewer in a newspaper or magazine. To perform any of the above is an infringement of copyright law.

Paperback Book: ISBN: 978-0-9869035-5-7
Ebook: ISBN: 9781502207937
Hardcover: ISBN: 9781312429666
Published MDHD Canada

Mallory Neeve Wilkins

Introduction

The mystical movement of energy.

The sacred studies of Feng Shui in China, Vaastu in India and geomancy elsewhere have for millennia mapped the path of the Earth's subtle energies. They have endeavored to bring harmony and well-being to people, buildings and the environment. In contrast to the antiquity of the sacred studies, modern scientific study of the Earth's energies is in its infancy.

These ancient traditions were once specific to their cultures, but over the last sixty years, they have found worldwide application in all aspects of architecture. Interest has spread with the realization that our environments are more toxic in both land and buildings and are suffering from geopathic stress.

Feng Shui and Vaastu Shastra are sacred, mysterious studies. They aim to create a healthier environment by balancing the flow of positive and negative energies.

***

PART I

CHINA – FENG SHUI

Feng Shui: The Ancient Art of Living in Harmony with the Environment

A house carries energy from the land, the architect, the builder, and everyone who worked on it or lives in it, and every 'thing' inside it.

Throughout history, we are consistently told that our basic need is to live in harmony within our environment. Our goal is to be able to create a space of well-being and prosperity, a healthy, comfortable place where your mind is at total peace. A place where you are revitalized, renewed and can be more creative. Everything that you see around your home gives off and takes on energy, so if there are things that you do not love, need or use regularly, you should consider getting rid of them … all of them.

Included in the following chapters are several Feng Shui calculations that will appear to be complicated. These once secret calculations, which date back thousands of years, are the way of mapping the energy flow within your environment. Feng Shui is all about feelings. The space must feel right for your particular needs.

For good Feng Shui living, focus on the 'feeling' of the space, and your inner self (intuition) will let you know if it is the correct chair to sit in, the right side of the bed to sleep on, the correct color to paint, the right room to eat in. You may know that you don't like it, but do you understand how to correct it?

When you feel anxious, restless, and not as healthy as you would like to be, then the building and the things in it may no longer be compatible. Perhaps you are a *West Person*, working or sleeping in an East (energy) room. It is all about analyzing your space, item by item and creating a place that 'feels' great, to achieve a healthy environment. By making certain corrections that will enhance your lifestyle, your health and your moods, you will become aware of good Feng Shui that attracts the flow of positive energy. Nature can be your guide.

***

FENG SHUI ALIGNMENT

- Alignment is for anyone who seeks 'corrections' in their life.
- There are Yin and Yang energies ~ East and West energies.
- A building is identified as either an East or a West structure, (depending on its placement and the direction it faces.)
- A person is identified as either an East or a West person, (depending on the year in which they were born.)
- Each year, the earth carries a different flow of energy. (Fire, water, metal, wood, earth exists in a flow of Yin or Yang energies.)
- To attract maximum positive energy, an East person should live in an East house. (Calculations made with a compass)
- Know your Home! First, identify its energy by how it 'sits' on the property.

***

Small Spaces ... Fashion & Feng Shui

- Whether you are setting up your first apartment, or your first home, it is usually going to be the smallest of all your homes, until you retire and then it turns into a matter of sheer downsizing.
- Designing any small space is no easy task, but the secret to great design is to remember that the main pieces of furniture in the room should blend into the wall color. Visually, this will create the feeling of walking through a larger space as the pieces of furniture blend into the background. This allows the energy to flow, meander throughout the space without an abrupt interruption. By coordinating the background color with the furnishings, it creates a restful room and allows the room to take on your personality.
- By changing the accessories from one theme to another (i.e. reds/greens to another of

black/whites) you are free to create a space suitable to your moods. A winter look and a summer look are accomplished by alternating your decorative pieces. You can select simple side-panel drapes, a floral arrangement and accent pillows that will transform the whole look of a small space - as long as the main larger furnishings blend into the background wall color.

- In Feng Shui design, remember to keep your pillows (on your small sofa) to one side, always allowing empty space on the other side for new positive energy to enter. This also reduces visual clutter.
- The purpose of installing full-length drapes is to heighten the space. Drapes provide the room with a more complete look, without that 'not quite finished' appearance. There are several options for drapes - from plain or textured fabrics in the same color tone as the wall color, or select patterned and striped fabrics that contain the shades from your room's color palette.
- The main concern is to make sure that whatever fabric you have selected for your window dressing should also be placed elsewhere in the room, such as, on matching pillows, a chair slipcover, upholstery pieces, ottoman or even a lampshade. The coordination of fabrics will help in creating a balanced room with a sense of continuity. Keeping things simple, without being monochromatic, will carry your personality into the space.

Small rooms: specifications you will need to know when making a purchase. Recommendations:

- Loveseat/sofa suggested measurements: 68"Wide x 30"Back-Height x 36"Depth
- Two accent chairs = 30"W x 36"D x 30"BH
- Small Coffee tables = 36" oval, round or square
- Side-panel drapes = single-width panel of lined fabric 54"wide, floor length
- Art groupings = 2 ½ inch space between items
- Lamps = tri-lites (one switch with three light options)
- Walls = ivory, pastels, gray, beige, white, neutral

Rules for Small Spaces.

Observe the lighting in the room.
Light intensity represents fire-energy and keeps the energy moving. Windows, lamps, candles and skylites are all examples of this element, which is required for uplifting energy.

Keep the room bright as heavy window dressings can block out the flow of positive energy, so it is important to consider the function of the room before selecting a specific covering. If privacy is a concern, always list your needs/options before purchasing to make sure you will be comfortable with your final decision.

Tri-lites are recommended for all lamps, whether floor or table models for your multi-tasking options.

A large range of designs and styles of lamps and candles are sold online, in department stores, boutiques and lighting stores.

Each purchase should be considered carefully so you

do not select an item that you happen to fall in love with but it doesn't suit the room style. The more care you take in putting your pieces together, the more prosperous will be the energy flow.

Furniture and its placement.
Space planning can open or close the flow of incoming energy. Straight lines allow the energy to move too fast and not recommended, causing anxiety and restlessness, whereas placing some pieces of furniture on angles will slow down the flow, and create a 'meandering' movement. Never block incoming flow as this will create a negative effect, rejection. One should draw a plan of the room before spending hard-earned money on furnishings that you expect to last many years. Scale is balance. Balance is harmony.

Well-proportioned items enhance a relaxing atmosphere, and the fewer pieces there are, then the larger and less cluttered a room becomes. An empty room is full of positive energy. This good energy is reduced by each item that is placed within it. This means the occupant receives less of this good energy when adding more items and furniture. Less is best for a healthy home.

Consider the flooring.
Hard elements such as ceramic, tile, marble and slate carry earth-energy, while softer elements like cork, bamboo and hardwood carry wood-energy. Sometimes you have to use what is already in place, but covering it with a rug can provide you with options for accessorizing your room.

Color for small rooms can be tricky.
Softer tones are recommended. When deep shades are requested, place them on an accent wall, or on the lower sections of the walls that have been designed with a chair-rail. Finishes are very important. Velvet and suede paint *finishes* calm the flow of energy while a gloss surface encourages a faster flow of energy. Also, remember that latex paint is for drywall and oil-base paint is for plaster walls. When switching from one type to another, always apply a primer-sealer before your finish coat of paint.

Accessory items.
Keep your tables clear from clutter by using two or three items (should be ample), leaving at least fifty percent of the surface empty for new energy to flow into your life.
Placing objects and artwork on your walls or bookshelves should appear as a collection of special items that you are fond of, not just 'things' that fill the space. It is better to leave walls empty than to hang pieces that are not loved, as they should represent prosperity. Items not cared for, soiled, cracked, broken or damaged convey neglect. This impression has a negative effect on the prosperity aspiration.

***

A Small Condo Gets a Facelift

This special Vancouver condo has a tiny living room space area of only 128 sq ft. To create a sense of harmony and balance for the fashion-conscious homeowner, a mono-chromatic color scheme was selected (black and cream) to combine the traditional furniture with a modern outlook.

The small space lacked storage, which was overcome by selecting a large ottoman that opened up for multi uses, and had a Naugahyde finish for durability. The large surface provided ample space as a coffee table unit.

Three decorative drapery panels designed to break-up and enhance the floor-to-ceiling windows created a unique backdrop stage for the comfortable seating and media area.

Too much glass within a unit such as a high-rise condo can cause vulnerability... but selective window coverings can reduce this effect.

Neutral walls, sofa and carpeting were topped with basic accessories. The Feng Shui meandering placement of furnishings allows positive energy to flow into the space.

Always place a life element such as plants, flowers or a tree in the Southeast corner to encourage prosperity in the wealth sector of the room. The silk tree placed in this sector of the room was seven feet tall.

A wise homeowner knows to encourage positive energy with splashes of red in the South and Southwest sectors of a room for strong relationships. A lampshade in red silk and a complementary oversize candle was selected for the second item as it is recommended that <u>two red items</u> be located in the Relationship sector, and the vase of flowers encourages growth by carrying the energy of wood, which enhances 'fire' energy of this sector.

Accent chairs must be comfortable since there is limited room for large upholstered pieces in a small space. The fabric selected for the window treatment mimicked the open-arm occasional chair. This illustrates continuity, which is an important part of Feng Shui. A large man-size wing chair placed in the corner of the room provided comfortable seating.

If you remove all the accessories, you're left with

antique white blinds, white walls and white carpet with a white sofa. This clean, neutral palette can be made to look different each time you get a change-of-heart and want to replace your accessories, making it possible to go from a Dutch-blue/white, to pastel florals or a dramatic bold masculine décor.

***

Color
The use of color is an expression of one's energy.

Special rooms require attention-to-detail, and the use of bold textures and colors can accomplish this effect.

Red is 'supportive' when used in the Northeast and Southwest rooms and in the South. It is not wise to have too much red in the North because it can attract loss and difficulties in the Career Sector.

Red is not a color you should use in a bedroom or any room in which you spend a great deal of time. It creates high energy and could result in you feeling exhausted.

***

Guest Room

Spice up a guest room by developing a 'theme' and use color, such as, creating a theme with a simple rattan headboard for the bed.

Add accent (animal) pillows, decorative lamps, wooden blinds that are the same wood-tone color as the headboard and add some 'theme' wallpaper to complement the fabrics selected for the bedding.

Consider the use of hardwood for the floors, if your budget permits.

Create a fun space.

***

Small bedrooms

Small rooms enhanced by painting the headboard wall the same color as the bedcover will delicately blend the two together.

By using this same color, the room appears larger. Also apply this color to the outside window frame and other features such as the baseboards and doorframes in the room. Add some whimsy with decorative, bold pillows and shams on the bed.

A custom headboard inexpensively created by padding a decorative board and adding bold accent piping, buttons and multi-colored textured fabric, which will coordinate all the features of the room.
Do not place anything over the head of the bed, such as artwork or other decorative pieces, especially mirrors.
Keep the bedroom calm and free of clutter.

Dining Areas

It is said in Feng Shui, you should never eat where the food is being prepared. A separate area is required for eating.

Dressing-up a small dining space with long, colorful lined drapes, a large mirror and unique accessories can change a bland corner into an attractive area.

A mirror over the table multiplies the prosperity of the owner's abundance by doubling the reflection of food, its nurturing and healing effects.

Colorful chair upholstery with gold-script lettering adds sparkle for a sense of whimsy and richness.

Add a 'life' element to the room with colorful plants or flowers, keeping them healthy and displayed with care, representing growth and good health.

'Earth' elements recommended for the center of the table are crystal, china or pottery; it will impart a sense of being grounded, or being centered.

If the overhead-light location is not centered over the table, change the ceiling fixture from a chandelier style to one that sits tighter to the surface.

The seating around the table where you eat must be comfortable with a high, well-supported back. Relaxation at meal times aids in a good digestive system and a harmonious flow of positive energy.

Round tables considered free from poison arrows, or pointed edges, aid in the flow of positive energy.

Small spaces can accommodate dining areas by using a drop-leaf table, which can be multi-functional. When not used for eating, the table folds, tucks away or placed against a wall, which visually opens up the space.

***

Don't forget the Garage

Take a close look at the location of your garage and what is inside it. The location could be in the Wealth Aspiration (SE) or Relationship Aspiration (SW) or Health Aspiration (E). If there are weaknesses or problems in these areas of your life... take a closer look.

Large tools left unorganized represents weapons and carry the negative energy of poison arrows ... not good for relationships. The garage is a place for specific storage, handiwork, creative ventures and maybe collectibles. Not everyone has a space large enough to savor their gardening tools, automobiles, hockey 'Gretzky' memorabilia or life-long photo gallery, but whatever is in this sector might be affecting your personal energy. If you don't use or enjoy certain items, the garage becomes an enlarged garbage bin.

Vehicles, tools and machinery represent metal-energy. If the garage is located in the East or Southeast sector, then there will be loss and mishaps in the areas of health and finances because E and SE carry wood-energy and *metal cuts wood*. The metal items are best placed in the West and Northwest sections of the garage. It is also wise to have windows or skylites in this space for good light (fire-energy).

Paint the ceiling of the garage white and the walls in a shade of beige/tan to keep things grounded and bright.

Always keep the floor clutter-free so as not to bring impurities into your home.

A 'working' garage should carry a sense of humor (poster, memorabilia etc) so as not to lose focus when there has been a bad day.

Play your favorite music to enhance creativity and keep a good mood.

Keep the space junk-free so that unused 'things' don't become stagnant, carry negative energy, and attract unwanted issues into your life.

Keep the entrance door clear of storage to allow positive energy to enter and ward off mishaps, anxiety and loss.

~A~
Identifying an East and West House

The reason you need to determine the building's location is to find out if you are compatible or need to make corrections. An East person lives and works better in an East building creating an even flow of energies. A certain feeling of comfort is experienced when everything is in harmony. An East House is one that 'sits' in the N, S, SE, or E.

To identify the entry ... you will need to stand and face the main entrance door of the building from the inside, looking out – and determine its direction with a compass. The opposite side of the compass (to this direction) will identify how the structure sits, which names its location. If the front door faces South (direction) on the compass when you look out the main entrance, then the opposite position on the compass would be North, therefore the building sits in a North location. A little complicated, but energy is known to meander.

East building locations are those that sit North, South, Southeast and East. (Therefore, their directions when facing out the main entrance are those on the opposite side, which would be: South, North, Northwest and West.) The 'perfect' East House would be one that sits and faces – North / South.

West building locations are those that sit West, Northeast, Southwest and Northwest. (Therefore, their directions are those facing the opposite: East, Southwest, Northeast and Southeast.) The 'perfect' West House would sit and face Northeast / Southwest.

The purpose of aligning the compass is to determine:
 1 -The eight Aspiration locations for each room of the building.
 2 -The five elements required to enhance the energy.
 3 -The colors used to create positive energy.
 4 -The shapes and patterns used to reduce negative energy.
 5 -The placement of the products and materials in each room.
 6 -The best door for you to enter to bring positive energy into the building.

Details for the Aspirations
Career, Relationships and Health

The following information will allow you to be specific in your own needs as to how to set up your space for well-being, prosperity and a revitalized lifestyle. Feng Shui realignment of energy can be done by obtaining....

- a compass
- a floor plan of the building/home
- the birthdates of anyone living or working in the building
- five items: natural elements (wood, water, metal, fire, earth)

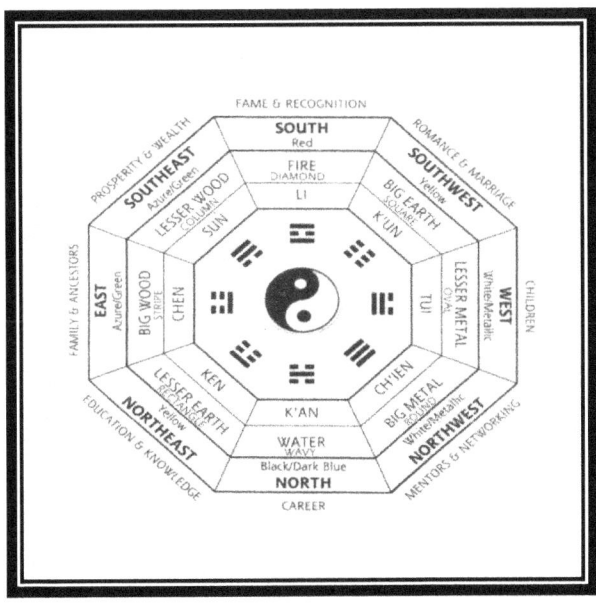

~ B ~
There are eight sectors that carry an Aspiration (Compass Tradition).

Pa Kua NUMBER, its LOCATION and its ASPIRATION

1. North - Career
8. Northeast - Knowledge
3. East - Health and Family
4. Southeast - Wealth
5. Centre
9. South - Recognition
2. Southwest - Relationship
7. West - Creativity and Children
6. Northwest - Friendships and/or Travel

(These Pa Kua numbers are identified on the **Lo Shun** square.)

Place a compass over your plan/drawing of the house, apartment or place of business and designate <u>where</u> the above Aspirations are located on <u>your</u> plan. You are interested in knowing where the wealth (SE) and health (E) Aspirations are situated because you don't want them to fall into a location of negative energy such as the garage or bathroom as these areas carry 'negative *sha ch'i* energy'.

A Chinese compass needle will point to South, while a North American compass needle points to North.
Identify each location/sector of your floor plan with the correct Aspiration.

For example, your main entrance could be the Relationship Aspiration because it was located in the SW sector of the building. The bathroom could be in the Friendships Aspiration area because it was located in the NW sector of the building causing loss in the specific area of these Aspirations.

***

~ C ~
Identify the Energy within a Building

The natural (environmental) energy carried by each sector of the compass.

Feng Shui: the mystical movement of an invisible energy, which vibrates throughout the environment (wind) as well as within your body (breath) ... and water.

A building carries energy from the land, the architect, the builder and everyone who worked on it or lives in it, and every 'thing' inside it. Be aware of these facts.

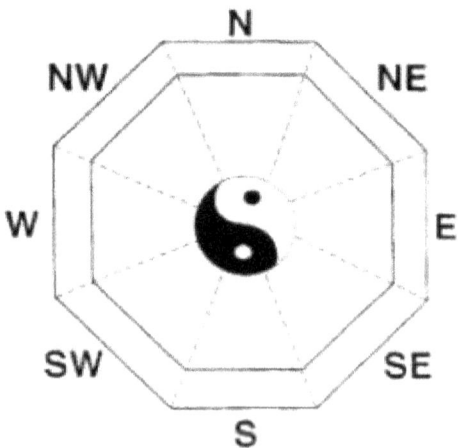

The compass has eight sectors. N NE E SE S SW W NW There are eight different energy vibrations within the compass field (locations) and there are eight individual Aspirations that carry their own colors and shapes, which identify and encourage positive energy when used in their correct location.

- **The N North sector** (1)

carries the energy of water, the color dark, navy-black and the shape of irregular movement, the wave.

- **The NE Northeast sector (8)**

carries the energy of earth, the colors tan, yellow and brown, and the shape of square and rectangle.

- **The E East sector (3)**

carries the energy of the element wood, the color green-blue, and the shape of vertical, stripe or column.

- **The SE Southeast sector (4)**

Also carries the energy of wood, the color green, and the shape of vertical, stripe, and column.

- **The S South sector (9)**

of the compass carries the energy of fire, the colors red to pink and the shape of a triangle, diamond or pointed cone.

- **The SW Southwest sector (2)**

carries the energy of earth, the colors of yellow-orange to browns and the shape of a square or rectangle.

- **The W West sector (7)**

carries the energy of metal, the colors pastel, gray and white and the shape of oval or round.

- **The NW Northwest sector (6)**

likewise carries the energy of metal, the colors pastel, gray and white and the shapes of oval and round.

The colors, shapes and natural elements are what create and carry positive and negative energy fields, depending on their location. You can walk through a negative field and not even know it, and have a bad day.

***

~ D ~
PA KUA
For East & West persons
(Calculations from the birth year)

"How to find out if you are an East or West Person"

Calculations for a 'quick 'n easy' short cut...
For birth year **calculations up to year 2000...**
Instructions
Take your birth year – example 1977
Add the last 2 digits together: 7+7=14
Always reduce (add) to a single digit: 1+4=5

Male – subtract the 5 from 10 (10-5=5)
Female – add the 5 to 5 (5+5=10)
Always reduce (add) to a single digit (1+0=1)

Example Summary:
A male would is a West person with Pa Kua number 5
A female is an East person with Pa Kua number 1
Pa Kua Numbers:
1, 3, 4, 9 for East Persons
2, 5, 6, 7, 8 are West Persons

* SPECIAL NOTE: There is no number 5 as it represents the center of the compass.
A male 5 would actually be a 2 and a female 5 would be an 8. (See the following charts on directions.) These accurate calculations are important when calculating your personal four best locations (to be situated in) for surrounding yourself with positive energy, for sleeping, eating, working etc.

If you were born between Jan 1 and March 1 consult the Chinese calendar (see section F) to confirm your 'correct' birth year' for these calculations to be accurate.

After the year 2000 ...all calculations changed.

Make special note of the changes in making calculations. To get the needed results after 2000, it now means that birth years of the Male will need to subtract from 9, while Female birth years will now have to add to 6 when making calculations to obtain the Pa Kua number.

Interesting Note:

The Chinese compass identifies South at the top. (Fire-South over Water-North ~ sun over ocean), while the North American compass identifies North at the top (Water over Fire ~ clouds/rain drown/put-out fire).

See the following chart.

***

~ E ~

Best & Worst Energy Directions & Locations
Based on your personal Pa Kua Number

'A-D' good energy locations   **'X-0'** poor energy areas

Pa Kua #	A	B	C	D	X	Y	Z	'0'
1	SE	E	S	N	W	NE	NW	SW
2	NE	W	NW	SW	E	SE	S	N
3	S	N	SE	E	SW	NW	NE	W
4	N	S	E	SE	NW	SW	W	NE
5-M	NE	W	NW	SW	E	SE	S	N
5-F	SW	NW	W	NE	S	N	E	SE
6	W	NE	SW	NW	SE	E	N	S
7	NW	SW	NE	W	N	S	SE	E
8	SW	NW	W	NE	S	N	E	SE
9	E	SE	N	S	NE	W	SW	NW

~ F ~
Dates of the Chinese New Year

Sample: If you were born January 30, 1938, (30.01.38) then your environmental birth element 'energy' would be in 1937 – (Yin Fire energy) because the new year does not begin until the January 31.

31.01.1938	Yang Earth	Tiger
19.02.1939	Yin Earth	Hare
08.02.1940	Yang Metal	Dragon
27.01.1941	Yin Metal	Snake
15.01.1942	Yang Water	Horse
05.02.1943	Yin Water	Sheep
25.01.1944	Yang Wood	Monkey
13.02.1945	Yin Wood	Rooster
02.02.1946	Yang Fire	Dog
22.01.1947	Yin Fire	Boar
10.02.1948	Yang Earth	Rat
29.01.1949	Yin Earth	Ox
17.02.1950	Yang Metal	Tiger
06.02.1951	Yin Metal	Hare
27.01.1952	Yang Water	Dragon
14.02.1953	Yin Water	Snake
03.02.1954	Yang Wood	Horse

24.01.1955	Yin Wood	Sheep
12.02.1956	Yang Fire	Monkey
31.01.1957	Yin Fire	Rooster
18.02.1958	Yang Earth	Dog
08.02.1959	Yin Earth	Boar
28.01.1960	Yang Metal	Rat
15.02.1961	Yin Metal	Ox
05.02.1962	Yang Water	Tiger
25.01.1963	Yin Water	Hare
13.02.1964	Yang Wood	Dragon
02.02.1965	Yin Wood	Snake
21.01.1966	Yang Fire	Horse
09.02.1967	Yin Fire	Sheep
30.01.1968	Yang Earth	Monkey
17.02.1969	Yin Earth	Rooster
06.02.1970	Yang Metal	Dog
27.01.1971	Yin Metal	Boar
15.02.1972	Yang Water	Rat
03.02.1973	Yin Water	Ox
23.01.1974	Yang Wood	Tiger
11.02.1975	Yin Wood	Hare
31.01.1976	Yang Fire	Dragon
18.02.1977	Yin Fire	Snake
07.02.1978	Yang Earth	Horse

28.01.1979	Yin Earth	Sheep
16.02.1980	Yang Metal	Monkey
05.02.1981	Yin Metal	Rooster
25.01.1982	Yang Water	Dog
13.02.1983	Yin Water	Boar
02.02.1984	Yang Wood	Rat
20.02.1985	Yin Wood	Ox
09.02.1986	Yang Fire	Tiger
29.01.1987	Yin Fire	Hare
17.02.1988	Yang Earth	Dragon
06.02.1989	Yin Earth	Snake
27.01.1990	Yang Metal	Horse
15.02.1991	Yin Metal	Sheep
04.02.1992	Yang Water	Monkey
23.01.1993	Yin Water	Rooster
10.02.1994	Yang Wood	Dog
31.01.1995	Yin Wood	Boar
19.02.1996	Yang Fire	Rat
07.02.1997	Yin Fire	Ox
28.01.1998	Yang Earth	Tiger
16.02.1999	Yin Earth	Hare
05.02.2000	Yang Metal	Dragon
24.01.2001	Yin Metal	Snake
12.02.2002	Yang Water	Horse

01.02.2003 Yin Water   Sheep
22.01.2004 Yang Wood   Monkey
09.02.2005 Yin Wood   Rooster
29.01.2006 Yang Fire   Dog
18.02.2007 Yin Fire   Boar
02.02.2008 Yang Earth   Rat
26.01.2009 Yin Earth   Ox
14.01.2010 Yang Metal   Tiger
03.02.2011 Yin Metal   Hare
23.01.2012 Yang Water   Dragon
10.02.2013 Yin Water   Snake
31.01.2014 Yang Wood   Horse
19.02.2015 Yin Wood   Sheep
08.02.2016 Yang Fire   Monkey
28.01.2017 Yin Fire   Rooster
16.02.2018 Yang Earth   Dog
05.02.2019 Yin Earth   Boar
25.01.2020 Yang Metal   Rat
etc

When you are reading the above list, note that the date listed is the *first day* of the Chinese year and it ends the day before the date listed below it (in the column on the left side).

~ G ~
PA KUA NUMBERS
(Positions on the Lo Shun)

SOUTH		
Wood **4** Green	Fire **9** Red	Earth **2** Yellow
Wood **3** Green	Earth **5** Yellow	Metal **7** White/Metallic
Earth **8** Yellow	Water **1** Black/Dark Blue	Metal **6** White/Metallic

This Square contains numbers, colors and elements of the **Lo Shun**. The MAGIC SQUARE is where all the numbers add up to **15** or 1+5=6, vertically, horizontally and diagonally (6+6+6=18=9) New beginnings & insight. This 'square' information represents your Inner spiritual-energy and intuition based on the calculations from your birth year (pa kua) while your Outer (environmental) is the energy the 'earth' carries in the year you were born which represents body-energy. Are you more spiritual-intuitive or materialistic-physical?

Nine is a magic number representing rebirth, perfection, eternal, full circle.

~ H ~
Your energy carried from Earth.

How to calculate your 'earth energy' that you carry with you all the days of your life.

SHORT-CUT CALCULATIONS

Example: based on the Chinese calendar on previous page

Take the year you were born - 1977
Take the **last digit** of the year - 7
The year 1977 carries the energy of Yin fire.

Odd numbers carry YIN energy. 1, 3, 5, 7, 9
Even numbers carry YANG energy. 0, 2, 4, 6, 8

The last digit of the year you were born indicates your Earth's energy.

- 0 – YANG - METAL
- 1 – YIN - METAL
- 2 – YANG -WATER
- 3 – YIN - WATER
- 4 – YANG - WOOD
- 5 – YIN - WOOD
- 6 – YANG - FIRE
- 7 – YIN - FIRE
- 8 - YANG - EARTH
- 9 – YIN - EARTH

~ 1 ~
ENVIRONMENTAL ENERGY CHART
Enhancement & Control

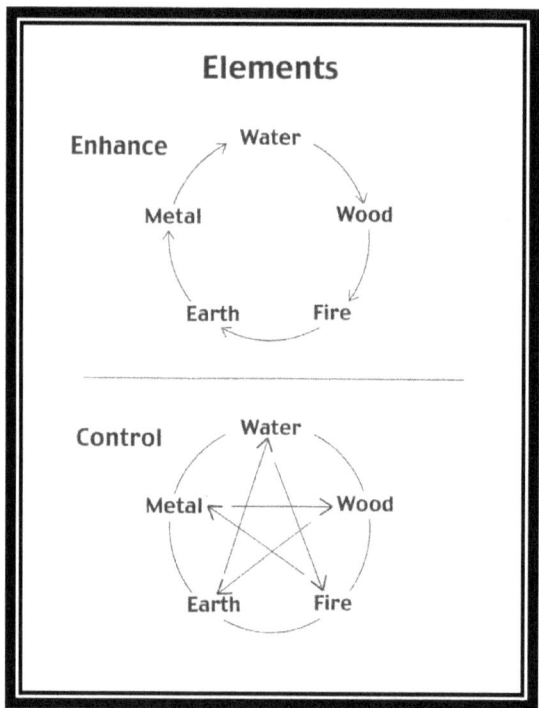

- Water Wood Fire Earth Metal – natural elements
- Each year the earth carries a different energy from one of the five different natural elements.
- All your life you carry this outer energy, calculated from your birth-year.

- The **element** from your birth year has support from other elements to enhance your energy when you need a boost, and others that control it when things get out of hand.

- Each element is represented by a color, shape and material. These items improve the energy within your environment and create balance, and a sense of well-being.

***

FENG SHUI APPLICATIONS
(FOR TRADITIONAL COMPASS SCHOOL)

Creating positive energy in
the area of
'Career'

Aspiration
'Career' can be looked at as 'an individual's course or progress through life'. It usually pertains to a person's path ~ a journey that makes up a person's occupation.

The origin of the term comes from the Latin word carrera, which means race (as in rat race, a pejorative implying the opposite of a useful career).

"Career" in the 20th century refers to the series of jobs or positions by which one earns one's money. It also refers to an individual's work and life role over his or her lifespan.

North sector is 'always' the location for enhancing the aspiration, Career. Wherever you conduct your business, your office or workspace, it can vary widely depending on the location of the room within the building where you work. But, the 'North area' in every room is the Career aspiration sector. Water is the element for North. In general, a good Feng Shui office design can greatly improve a person's productivity, business success, and attract prosperity.

Office Specifications
If a person's life's journey is the aspiration 'Career', then where is the best location in the home to set up an

office, place of work, area for study or creative space?
North (career) East Person
Southeast (wealth) East Person
Northeast (knowledge) West Person
Northwest (friendships) West Person

- The absolute worst locations for the workspace are in the center of the house, in the bedroom, or under a stairway.
- There are two choice locations within the home for both East and West persons. The best office location for the East person would be North; and the best location for the office for a West person would be Northeast. But, there are four prosperous locations that carry positive energy for each person.
- Feng Shui recommends that a person's career area be separate from the rest of the house. The best option would be a completely separate room with a window.
- Try to use a separate entrance to your office.
- A room with a low ceiling is not the best option: it provides too little space for a person's potential to develop and grow, whether creative or business.
- If your office space has to be part of another room, divide the designated space from the rest of the room with a screen or large planters.
- Business meetings held in a home office need a separate entrance to the room. The shortest distance through your house is for the better.
- Seven design elements need considering: flooring, walls, windows, lighting, furnishings, color

and space planning. They all affect the flow of energy and can have an effect on the productivity, not to forget the creativity.

- When there are doorways of offices that face one another across a hallway, place a small round or square mirror (depending on its direction) on the front of each door. This alters the flow and can make immediate corrections when needed.
- If you face a partial wall or partition when entering an office, place a mirror on the partition.

Setting up a home Office.
Where and how to begin to put things together.

Once the location has been selected for your workspace, draw a plan of the room on a large paper. Identify 'carefully' the exact placement of all the following items:
doors, closets, windows, corner walls, alcoves, bays and sharp angles, plugs and outlets and skylites.

Identify the following areas in your room by overlaying a diagram of the compass. Be precise.

1. The eight compass locations (North, West, Southeast etc)
2. The eight aspirations (career, friendships, knowledge etc)
3. Four best locations for the desk = make sure your back does not face the entry.
4. Prepare and space-cleanse the room with a

five-element cleansing kit (wood, fire, water, metal and earth) to music that you love. Sound will activate the energy with your input.
5. Don't place your desk under a window unless the window has been covered, and let the light reflect through it. Some people prefer to have their desks facing East.
6. The work-desk is to be located in an area where there is good lighting and near a window.
7. Setting up the space for the office must include a thorough wash of the windows and walls to refresh the space. Paint or decorate with paper whenever possible.
8. Nothing cracked, broken or damaged should be in the office.

Placement options:

According to 'office Feng Shui guidelines', place your desk at a diagonal to the doorway or directly facing it. You should not sit with your back to the doorway.
Place your desk on the corner diagonally opposite the doorway. Don't cramp your style by having a work surface not large enough for your needs.

For offices that contain more than one desk, place two on a diagonal facing toward the door and any others on a diagonal facing into the center of the room. They should NOT be placed in rows in a traditional classroom layout, nor should their users sit back to back creating a **conflict of energies.**

Room size and desk size should complement each other and not be too small or too large.

Leave a small space between your furniture and the walls. Feng Shui experts suggest leaving a 5-inch gap from the wall for the energy to meander, circulate, and leave open spaces on bookcases so not to create stagnant energy.

**

Desk and Work Surfaces
A few suggestions regarding the items and their placement in the workspace.

East person
(wood, water and fire enhancing elements)
- wood, black or mahogany desk, or green stained surface
- teal, red-burgundy or green colored materials
- L-shape; U-shape (irregular) shape for work desk

West person
(earth and metal enhancing elements)
- metal desk or a top surface of marble, granite, ceramic
- brown surface, or pastel, gray, white or light colored materials
- round, square or rectangular shape surface for workspace

The office furniture should be new so as not to carry or bring forward old energies that might be negative. If you have to use a second-hand work surface, make sure it has been cleaned, repaired and resurfaced or freshly painted.

Begin by clearing out. You want an empty palette.

Lighting

A lamp (fire element energy) is recommended for the South, Southwest or Northeast corner of the desk.
A tri-lite bulb (3-way switch) lamp offers the best solution.
A floor lamp can solve a difficult problem if there is not adequate space on the work surface. Never be in a room with a burned out bulb indicating neglect in your life. Never sit directly under an overhead light as they are considered fire energy and could cause headaches and indecision.

- No chips, marks, stains or other breaks showing

neglect on the surface or sides.
- Desks should be in excellent repair so as not to attract negative work or situations. The drawers should operate with ease and the handles should be tight and firm – not loose or damaged.
- If there are open shelves, storage or cabinets nearby, nothing should ever be placed on top of them, but rather contained within the space. This area is kept clear for meandering positive energy to flow easily, without any obstruction that could cause negative energy flow.
- Closed or covered shelves are recommended over open shelves. Everything situated on the shelf should fit the space and not overlap the edges. Know the difference between clutter and storage.
- Stored items don't have to be catalogued and labeled but they should be stacked neatly in a cupboard or in binders so as not to impede energy flow. Have adequate storage to leave lots of space on your working surface ~ clarity.
- No loose papers. Be in control. Papers should be contained within a binder, basket, folder or tray so that the energy reaches the person and not the papers. If the papers are bills, parking tickets, charge cards creating negative energy, they will cause more adverse influences to come into the person's life.
- No broken pencils or pens. These represent neglect; unwanted negative issues will arise from items that are damaged, broken or cracked.
- Never have more items in view than you need or use as there is no room for new energy to settle.

Less is best for clarity and success.

- **Metal items**: place away in a container. Staplers, scissors, paper cutters, paper-hole punch and other such articles can be sharp representing poison arrows that cause the energy to change from positive to negative. Place phones on an alternative surface rather than on the main work desk.

Before and After Office Pictures

Balance

Everything must be organized, clean space with only what is being used in the moment visible, and the rest covered or hidden from surrounding energy while working.

Soften jutting corner walls (corners) with plants to keep the sharpness from pointing at you ~ representing poison arrows.

Easy, movable seating is suggested for flexibility and comfort. Adjustable seat heights, for ease of operation and portability for special needs, are a good investment.

Hide exposed wires or consider using laptops to limit metal energy.

Feng Shui elements that are easiest to blend into an office decor are pictures and photos. They should indicate prosperity.

Reduce wall art - only a few pieces to expose more space for personal clarity.

Always look for pictures that represent the various aspects of your 'journey' and display them.

Very obvious Feng Shui symbols might invite unwelcome questions from co-workers. Dragons, turtles and incense are not required elements.

Store boxes that are not being used in a closet or

special storage area away from the creative workspace. If items are not being used at the moment, put them away until they are needed.

No mirrored doors (too much movement) but wall mirrors can be enhancing. They should never face the entry door lest they reflect the positive energy out of the office.

A good high-back chair is recommended for support, comfort and protection. Select an adjustable, easily moved item that can blend into the decor and not stand out as an obvious distraction. Black or dark colors are not usually the best choice as they represent a large water-element in the center of the workspace. This can hinder continuity of creative thought.

***

Office, Counseling and Conversations.

- Cover the windows when the view is not inspiring but don't block out the light.
- Comfortable, relaxed-seating required for counseling and consulting.
- Keep the flooring neutral without patterns and the walls painted in a light color, not dark tones.
- Small viewing screen for required presentations.
- Adequate storage required for files and work supplies.
- Keep the room bright and spacious, but no open corners.
- Don't have your back to the door when working.
- Artwork is to be appropriate to the profession – degrees, awards, landscapes.
- An ottoman can be used for storage and a coffee table when selected in a color that matches the floor color, visually creating more space.

- Add greenery (life element & growth) which can be plants, flowers in a crystal vase or a silk bouquet.
- Furniture ~ use less ridged commercial items (in appearance) and no large patterned fabrics.
- Keep all unnecessary work, files and clutter out of view when consulting.

***

RENOVATIONS – updating

If someone is renovating, or creating a new space for the home office or place of work, the following elements are recommended in a West Room location.

West Sectors: NE – W – SW - NW
Flooring:
Stone, tile, marble, granite, terrazzo, aggregate, ceramic.
Stained wood: dark walnut or mahogany, or bleached pastel colors
Natural fiber carpets in light, colors, brown, tan, or yellow tones.
Walls: White, pastel colors or earth tones of beige to brown
Wallcoverings with round or square shapes, or a mixture of both
Windows:
Blinds or shades in metal, or white, neutral, light colors
Drapes in pastel fabrics with square or oval pattern

East Room Sectors: S – SE – N – E
Flooring:
Wood, cork, bamboo
Carpeting in darker tones, reds, charcoal & greens
Natural materials
Walls:
Dark colors gray, navy, and black
Medium shades of green, teal, and red
Paint or paper in stripes, wave or irregular shape pattern
Floral wallcoverings
Windows:
Drapery fabrics in plain colors or floral prints, irregular shapes, or flame patterns
Wood blinds or shades, textured woven materials

FENG SHUI
'CAREER' ENHANCEMENTS

The Northeast corner-area of the office is the recommended location for your personal inspirational items or books. This sector is for Knowledge. It is a good place to store things such as catalogs that relate to the work being done. This sector carries earth-energy where items of glass, marble, granite, crystal, stone and gems are enhancements and is a good area for students to study or keep their books as energy flows from these items. The room must remain in good order and tidy. Research material is kept in this area. Red is a good color to use to boost the energy when a correction is required.

The **Career** area of the office is the North sector and is suitable for black and white features when displayed as art, fabrics or decorative items. Anything to do with water is a very good element represented by seascapes, fountains, shells, sculptures of creatures from the sea, and other related items.

Make a mission statement as to where you want your career to take you, as this section is where you place your 'goals' or affirmations, mission statements with regard to your line of work. Be clear about your direction and the path you want to follow. If you are an artist and do work in stone, this is not the place for displaying them because earth-energy dams or dominates water-energy (see chart), so the enhancing energy of water (career) is weakened. Do not place any crystal or other gems in this area of the office. Metal objects are the enhancing energies.

Keep the windows clean so not to increase the risk of stagnant energy entering as it comes from the outside in. If the outlook is not to your liking, cover the window but still keep the light entering.

'Wealth' Area in a Feng Shui Office (SE)

Dress for success. Appear prosperous and have a healthy bamboo plant on your desk. (SE)

The Wealth aspiration is in the Southeast sector of a room. This is the area to enhance for prosperity, financial endeavors, abundance and increase. Wood is the enhancing energy.

Artwork should be prosperous, a good investment and ones that are truly loved.

Place a picture of a lake, waterfall or any other water scene on one of the walls in your wealth corner. Wood frames or the color green for its framing is recommended.

Water represents energy flow, movement of the space. Always be ready for 'new' to come.

Use an aquarium or small fountain if you prefer, next to greenery.

For growth, place a green smooth-leafed plant (e.g. jade plant) on a shelf in this corner. You can substitute an artificial silk plant if you tend to neglect live ones.

The allusion to growing wealth is obvious.

Avoid crowded surfaces or countertops (50% empty) to attract positive energy, finances, jobs and friendships.

Place other symbols of wealth in the SE corner. They can include some of the following ideas:

***

Helpful tips for (ancient) wealth prosperity.

1. Place a red envelope or silk fabric containing several coins next to a wood item.
2. Three Chinese coins tied with a red silk ribbon next to a plant.
3. A wheel or bell representing power in green and black.
4. A symbol or picture of red fish symbolizing wealth.
5. A lotus flower symbolizing great achievements from humble beginnings in a decorative jar of water near the entrance to your office.

***

The Aspiration 'Relationships'

Relationship – a state of connectedness; an association between two or more people that may range from fleeting to enduring; an emotional intimacy.

Southwest:
Relationship Aspiration is always located in the sector of Southwest. The energy represented in this sector is the element of earth represented by natural products: gemstones, marble, granite, stone, pottery, china, crystal, brick, glass, rock and slate.

When you are considering a correction to a personal relationship, whether it has to do with your sister, co-worker, parent, partner, friend or a pet, it is recommended that you state your problem as well as your wishes for betterment. Each situation needs its own correction and therefore you need to think about one relationship at a time.

If you are bothered by repeated, annoying calls from an old friend and the disruption causes anxiety, headaches, change of attitude or anger, then list the needs to make the relationship work. If you have tried blocking the caller's phone number, and a sincere verbal effort has been made to relieve the stress, then change the energy in the SW (Relationship) sector. The aspiration Relationship can be damaging to one's health because the strongest of all negative energies is

stress from unresolved situations.

Whether you are searching for that special friend or need to resolve an argument, the 'Relationship Aspiration' is usually the first of the eight aspirations to be corrected.

The Aspiration-energy and its location within a building or room are broken down by sector (location) into the following list.

NORTH - Career Energy
NORTHEAST - Knowledge Energy
EAST – Health / Family Energy
SOUTHEAST - Wealth Energy
SOUTH - Recognition Energy
SOUTHWEST - Relationship Energy
WEST – Creativity / children Energy
NORTHWEST - Friendships-travel Energy

A second sector can be enhanced if the relationship is geared to a specific individual. For example: A parent may have concerns regarding their son or daughter; therefore the West (Children Aspiration) sector may carry negativity and could be enhanced as well as the SW (Relationships Aspiration). Or if there is a concern regarding one's parents, then the East (Family Aspiration) sector could be enhanced.

There are different complications within every situation. Relationships need to be clearly visualized if the problem persists, and pictures are recommended for the way you would like the situation to look like, such as a plane flying away from your city with that annoying person on it.

The SW Relationship Aspiration is mainly the sector corrected for romance.
The Relationship **area** of a home is one that should be treated with exceptional care.

There are situations that involve family members, work co-harts, friends, team-sports members, siblings, children, neighbors, new acquaintances, romantic partners, etc.
When you are interested in making a 'correction' or want to attract a new relationship, then there are different applications for each need. If your interest is in a new partner, then five pillows on your bed is not the way to go. Consider two so you don't attract 'others' into the relationship.

If there is dissension in the work force, then specific applications need to be conceived. To solve the dilemma, express your intention in writing, then add the color red to the sector.

Make sure you situate yourself in your best location for eating, sleeping and working ... attracting positive energy to yourself at all times.
Some additional corrections to consider are:

- Keep two crystals in the Southwest window.
- Powerful change occurs from cleaning out closets and drawers. Make sure the garage is orderly and clean. It could be in your

- relationship, health or wealth area. No room for obstacles.
- When there are quarrels, mishaps and problems, take a look in the Southwest sector for any pointed-leaf plants, bookshelves, floral drapes, the color green, stripe wallpaper or water art, bouquets or flower arrangements, as these items attract negative energy.
- A basic Feng Shui cure for *sha ch'i* is a crystal. It can break the dark cloud of negative energy into thousands of sparkling little pieces of light.
- Make sure there is room for a partner to come/move into the home.
- Unblock communications by simply telling the truth, using "I" statements.

The best room to sleep in is selected by 'how it feels' even if the architecture of the home has dictated differently. The energy affecting the body is anywhere from six to ten hours of consecutive use. This space must be harmonious. It must be especially clean for clear-headedness. It must be filled with environmentally friendly materials (organic-natural) for the best sleep possible.

***

Enhance your accessories

- Place large items in twos (couple) in the Southwest sector of a room.
- Items such as two pieces of art, two large items with a lamp (representing fire), are an enhancement to the earth sector.
- Flowers represent growth, especially when placed on a section of red silk fabric.
- Use humor to deflect negative energy. In relationships humor can act like a crystal and transform tension into laughter.
- In Classical Feng Shui, Health & Relationships (aspirations) come first, because money (Wealth aspiration) can't buy good health and harmonious relationships.
- Are there problems within the family?
- Check the East sector of the house and the East corner of the living room. The East is the sector of Family Aspiration. If, for instance, there is a toilet in the East corner of the house, be sure to place

red items in here or paint the room red. Or, you can decorate in white and metal elements. As East is a wood-energy sector, the red (fire) and white (metal) energies will weaken the 'bathrooms negative energy'.

- Reds and metal colors exhaust the negative energy of the toilet when it is in the East sector. If there is a fireplace, then this will exhaust the relationships maybe through frequent arguments.
- A picture of water over the fireplace to drown the fire might be exhausting your family feelings.

The West sector is the Children aspiration.
If there are water elements in this area, such as a shower or bathroom, it can cause problems and difficulties with the children.

- Increase earth elements by placing vases or beautiful stones in the West corner of the living room, and to boost the children sector add metal vases, sculpture, or items in the color white.
- If there is a kitchen or a fireplace in the west, the water element is helpful, but so are earth elements, such as globes, maps, vases, or stones.
- Always check the center 'earth-energy' sector. This is a critical piece of the relationship puzzle. Without a strong center sector, health, wealth, and relationships can all suffer. Many homes are built with an open center creating a "hole in the heart" of the home, and can cause heartbreak and divorce as well as bankruptcy. Double this if

the home has a tree or plants growing in the center sector.
- The center sector is an earth sector. Plants - and especially trees - destroy earth and may have played a part in the break-up of Jennifer Anniston and Brad Pitt. (No courtyards allowed, with greenery in the center.)
- If the house has a kitchen in a center location, it can create severe disagreements and heated arguments. In this case, blue and black should be placed here as well as other water elements, such as an aquarium, fountain or fish-art (whales).

Many houses are irregularly shaped
with missing sectors. (SE - wealth; N – career etc) This can create problems with household members – especially if SW, NW or W is missing. Try to regularize the house and boost the missing sectors of your house by activating those sectors in the living room.

For a missing Southwest sector (romance, marital happiness, woman), Northwest sector (man, breadwinner), or West sector (children, creativity) add a globe to the space. They can be great "anchors" for the Southwest, Northwest, and West sectors.

This is a funny bit of Information... from a seminar I once took, they reported that socks represent a protective covering for your feet (a protection from external impurities) as you walk the pathway of life. Men and women often envision walking with their life partner forever together. Symbolically, by knotting one of their socks with the other's, in order to increase the probability of maintaining the long-term viability, enhances and knots the relationship. Feng Shui? ... Not sure about that one!

***

A successful 'Relationship' symbolism.

The artwork, color and grouping of objects can indicate what you want in life. What are you telling the universe you want out of a relationship? Clear out the clutter, single objects, family photos or that old chest and replace them with romantic images. Remember, how you set up the furniture in your room counts too. One nightstand and a bed against the wall suggest there is only room for one. (Bed should be five inches away from the wall.)

A combination of color, lighting and scents.

If you desire a healthy sex life, do not paint your bedroom lavender. This chaste energy is best left for your daughter's room until she is of an age to move out. Blue, yellow, brown and bright red are also problematic colors for the adult bedroom.

Think **romance** colors when you paint your bedroom and feel the sensuality in fabrics like cotton, silks, satin and chenille

.
- Spray your linens with some romantic aromas like Rose Bulgaria or Jasmine and ignite your inner passions. Top it off with some candles for soft lighting and you are ready for a long life of romance and passion.
- Place two roses along with a written list of the qualities you are looking for in a partner. Place a metal clock in the Northwest.
- Create a more relaxing yin environment by using

pale greens, blues, creams and other pastels along with natural materials like wicker and wood.
- What happens in bed stays in the bed.
- The bedroom is to be a place of Zen, so the vibrations are to remain soft and low for a good night sleep.
- Reading before sleep always helps. If this is a place for active, boisterous sex, the vibrations remain, linger, and can later be cause for restlessness and anxiety. Keep the high-energy lovemaking in a different room.
- An electric blanket is also considered a no-no (fire-metal energy).

***

Relationship Charts
(from previous chapters)

Figure out your personal Pa Kua number that can be computed by using your date of birth and sex. (Section D charts)

If your Pa Kua is 1, your 'relationship' direction is South.
If your Pa Kua is 2, your 'relationship' direction is Northwest.
If your Pa Kua is 3, your 'relationship' direction is Southeast.
If your Pa Kua is 4, your 'relationship' direction is East.
If your Pa Kua is 6, your 'relationship' direction is Southwest.
If your Pa Kua is 7, your 'relationship' direction is Northeast.
If your Pa Kua is 8, your 'relationship' direction is West.
If your Pa Kua is 9, your 'relationship' direction is North.

Example: As seen in Section E charts under column C.
A male born on 1st July 1957, your 'Kua' number is 7 and your 'relationship' direction is Northeast.
A female born on the 15th March 1977, your 'Kua' number is 1 and your 'relationship' direction is South.

How to apply the formula?

To improve your relationship luck, you should rearrange your table, chair and bed to face your 'relationship' direction. This can be your lucky corner.

The sleeping direction is taken from the crown of your

head. If your 'relationship' direction is North, then you should sleep with the crown of your head pointed at North and the base of your feet pointed South

Furnishings

Recommend soft lines relating to less hard, sharp edges in the West sector of a room, when there is a lot of communication taking place.

- Pillows: square shape for earth-energy; round shape for metal-energy; triangle, diamond, star shape for fire; ruffled shape for water-energy; and narrow-long shape for wood-energy.
- If you are married or in a relationship, it is recommended to hang pictures of the two of you together in the Southwest and Northwest.
- The headboard of the bed must be solid for long-lasting relationships. If you carry the energy of earth, a rectangle shape is recommended; Water-energy would use an irregular shape;

Metal-energy should be oval shaped headboard; Fire-energy is crown shape or pointed; Wood-energy would be vertical in shape.
- For couples, use a shape that would complement both of your elements and not one that might clash with your own element.
- Place a pair of objects in the Southwest corner.
- A few good examples of this would be a pair of Mandarin ducks or cranes as these are symbols of marital bliss.
- Another example is a heart-shaped figurine made from pink quartz crystal.
- Relocate any mirrors that face the bed because it reflects the couple on the bed. Some believe that this will cause a failure in the relationship because of the entry of a third party. Believe it or not, televisions are just as negative as mirrors, so remove them to prevent anxiety, headaches and indecision.
- Treat yourselves to fresh flowers, and once they wilt, replace them.
- Never put these in the Southwest corner of the room, as they will clash with the element of romance, namely earth. Flowers should only be placed in the East or Southeast and include the color red if located in the South.
- If there are any abstract, dark or sad artworks in the Southwest room, take them out. These things encourage negativity whereas the room should be peaceful and safe. You can replace them with a painting of peonies, lovebirds or silk flowers as all these represent love.

- The bedroom door - good repair and never squeak.
- A well-ventilated room moves out the old energy, keeping the space fresh and clean.
- Fix items in poor state of repair because they block romantic energy from entering the bedroom. This room must be in perfect condition and kept in good order with nothing under the bed.

Single people in need of relationship **corrections** can begin by making a wish list of what qualities they are looking for or would want in the ideal relationship. These are two different things and when you write it, be very specific. It may not happen today or tomorrow but one day, your ideal partner will show up.

Never make any changes or alterations to the room, home or office if things are going smoothly.

Work Relationships

Pay attention to your desk arrangement and make sure that your boss is situated 'at your back' so you are supported by this person. In the Northwest corner, place artwork with a mountain landscape in a gold frame.

- Activate your lucky corner. (as specified on previous pages). Place a photograph or description of your desired destiny on your desk. Again, don't sit with your back to the entry door.
- The fish and dragon symbols represent good luck when placed in the East.
- A desk in the Relationship area of Southwest

should not display anything that could represent 'hurt' such as scissors, stapler and remover, letter openers etc.
- Pink is a good accessory color or use small amounts of red. Avoid 'wood-energy' or the color green in this location. Two red roses are always acceptable. Earth element is the most enhancing.

Family relationships
This area can be activated in the wood-energy or East sector of a room by adding positive energy especially in the eating or dining room, or wherever the family gathers. Wood wind-chimes, family photos (in wooden frames) of happy times together, artwork of an English-country garden (full of color) all encourage positive energy.

When there is a lack of clear communication or misunderstanding, remove all past influences and items that may carry 'baggage' and negative energy, leaving the area clean.

Make the family and living areas of the house free of clutter and debris as only in places where there is no obstruction can there be positive energy flowing freely.

Any physical clutter in a room creates an obstacle in a person's mind and spirit. With its elimination, it is possible to make a family live happily together. Avoid using high-energy colors.
Display items that relate to the ancestry of the house to induce unity and help build a deeper connection.

Children's relationships

The West sector is Children Aspiration.
Metal is the element of choice, the color is white and round or oval are the enhancing shapes. If there are water elements in this area, such as a shower or bathroom, it can cause problems and difficulties with the children.

Increase earth elements in the home by placing vases or beautiful stones in the West area of the living room to boost the Children Aspiration. Also, add metal elements as well, such as metal vases or sculpture. This is not an area for fire-energy, so remove the red items, have good coverage for the windows, and cover any opening to the fireplace.

The child's bedroom and their study area are the most important energy-aspect of their development.
Posters with arrows, airplanes, weapons, hunting animals or angry scenes will not allow positive energy to flow. The study area should not be directly in front of a window lest concentration be disturbed.

Have lots of storage space to reduce clutter as it prevents a harmonious space for the children and causes stagnant or negative energy. The position of their beds is a health issue. Place beds in one of their best direction/locations, according to their personal energy charts.

Make sure there are no burnt-out lights, broken switch plates, squeaky doors or malfunctioning items, which can hinder their healthy growth. Their growth and learning skills can be stunted when children are surrounded by too many old items, so remove them for new things and let ideas come into their life. Less is always best.

One child per room will help the flow of energy, so if there is more than one per room, make sure they have completely separate areas. The mind, body and spirit need to stay healthy during growing years.

Stuck Relationships

Any relationship considered stuck should be observed closely. The aspiration may be located in an area of disharmony and poison arrows. Examine the space within the Relationship sector (SW) and notice if the energy is not flowing, or has nowhere to meander or move. Blocked or stagnant energy affects the mind when it is blocked in the environment. Open up a path and clear the area of any obstructions and a new clarity will be realized.

State your (relationship) intention and enhance the sector with corrections. Open the windows to encourage good lighting, use only natural products, clean off all surfaces on tables, desks and shelving areas.

Electronics must be in good working order. Play your favorite music.

Mallory Neeve Wilkins

PART II

INDIA - VAASTU SHASTRA

**The Science of
Construction ~ Architecture**

India Ancient Studies

Set down by Sages of the Vedic times, is one of the most ancient sciences of Indian architecture, composed of specific rules, regulations and directions known as Vaastu.

The word Vaastu derived from *'Vastoshpati'* used in the Rig-Veda, meant – provide protection, happiness and prosperity. Although the science of *Vaastu Shastra* evolved during *Treta Yug*, written evidence dates from a more recent 6,000 BC.

Indian Vaastu Shastra is the science of direction that combines all the five elements of nature, namely earth, water, air, fire and space and uses them to the benefit of mankind. It is the art of using these five elements also known as *Paanchbhootas,* for the prosperity of humans, connecting them to the world. Vaastu Shastra is an ancient Indian science of Vedic origin that deals with proper construction of a house.

Creating equilibrium between man and material.
It is said that as a science, it extracts the positive energy from the natural elements of the universe - the Paanchbhootas, namely, earth, water, air, sun and sky.

Vaastu Shastra aims at guiding construction
in such a way as to establish equilibrium, so that there is no hindrance to the flow of magnetic waves, from the North Pole to South Pole. It is believed that creating such a balance helps people avoid various calamities,

diseases and accidents, which might have occurred otherwise.

The principles of Vaastu

laid down in ancient times, were based purely on the effect of sunrays at different times of the day.

The word Vaastu stands for dwelling of humans and Gods over the ages.

According to Hindu practice, buildings should be constructed as per the directions mentioned in the Vaastu Shastra to attain complete harmony with natural forces for the well-being of humanity. The different directions and sectors of a house are assigned to different energies represented by ancient Gods and Guardians. These sectors, when constructed according to the nature of the God, lead to complete harmony and bring prosperity, good thought and sound health to people living inside.

Vaastu Shastra is well over 5000 years old

but since the 1990s there has been a sudden interest in the subject of the Vaastu Shastra. People seem to have rediscovered a long-lost panacea for their discomforts. All they need to do is make a few changes to their home or office layout and overnight, they have the health, wealth and happiness, which they lacked for so long.

Indian history has three distinct architectural epochs:
1. the Vedic (or Hindu) period
2. the Islamic period
3. the colonial period.

They are characterized by their respective myths and cultures.

In each time frame, structures were built that reflected the society of the time.

Intricately designed and sometimes complex temple structures, concerned with the mysterious and the metaphysical, are typical creations of the Hindu mind of ancient times. In contrast, simple rhythms and contemporary blank walls including the dominance of white color were attributes of Islamic culture and buildings.

The grandeur of power was reflected in the European architecture, while modern architecture in India has assimilated qualities of all three.

Buying a home in any city in India without the builder's following virtues of "Vaastu Shastra" and the project fulfilling Vaastu conditions is impossible. Over the last few decades, Vaastu Shastra has gained enormous popularity. Vaastu has found takers even among the most high and mighty of the land. Corporate leaders and politicians in power are constantly relocating and redesigning their offices according to this ancient science to see if it will improve their financial and political scorecards.

Natural Energies

Vaastu Shastra is based on various natural energies available in the atmosphere, namely:

Solar Energy
Lunar Energy
Earth Energy
Sky Energy
Electric Energy
Cosmic Energy
Magnetic Energy
Thermal Energy
Wind Energy
Light Energy

Energies were understood as vibrational frequencies.

The early principles of Vaastu
were framed from observation of the sunrays at different times in the day. These observations (mapping the path of the energies) were noted and important inferences drawn later on, on the basis of an in-depth screening. It is all about the equilibrium of the five elements (Earth, Water, Sun, Air & Space) in a building.

The vibrational frequencies of the land, and of each kind of material to be utilized, were compared to the natural resonance of a human being, and only the ones most beneficial for the purpose desired were used in the construction. Vaastu science pays close attention to the direction of underground water flows beneath a planned building site.

Five Elements

- Everything in this world is made of five elements. (earth, water, fire, air and space).
- The principles of Vaastu Shastra are mainly dependent on the arrangement of these elements.
- It is important to note that an imbalance of these elements in the Nature cycle can create calamities like earthquakes, volcanic eruptions, typhoons, tornadoes, floods or a famine.
- Such an imbalance can cause physical, mental or emotional upheaval in one's life.

Sun:
Sun is one of the most important elements of nature, on which our very survival depends. It is a source of heat and light, and therefore holds a lot of significance in the Vaastu study. The Sun, as our ancestors revealed, is the only source of light and heat for human and other living beings. It directs and sustains life on earth. Therefore, the rising Sun is considered sacred and is taken as a point of reference. If we face the rising sun, the facing direction is East, behind us is West, our left hand denotes North direction and right hand denotes South direction. The direction affects the building/house constructed therein.

Air:
Air, being the source of oxygen, acts as the lifesaver for human beings. The comfort level is dependent upon different things like airflow, air temperature, pressure, humidity level, etc. Air is one of the most powerful sources for our survival. It is a composition of gases like

oxygen, nitrogen, carbon dioxide, helium, neon, crypton and water vapor. Oxygen is a life-saving gas indispensable to living organisms.

Earth:
In India, earth is given the status of mother. It is the source of landforms, landscape, flora and fauna. The gravitational force and magnetic effects of Earth have an effect on living beings. It was formed about 460 crore ago (crore is ten million years) as a fiery ball. In due course, the rocks melted and the surface formed and acquired magnetism due to the magnetic particles embedded within. Earth has two poles, North and South.

Water:
Water is essential for the existence of all vibrational forms ~ animal, vegetable and mineral. In the past, human civilizations flourished around rivers and major waterways. Water has been used by humans for agriculture, drinking, by itself and in mineral solutions. Rainwater flowed into low-lying areas of earth's surface where oceans formed. The eternal water cycle is considered a mystery of nature.

Sky:
The sky consists of not just our solar system, but also the other galaxies that form a part of it. It provides a shelter to all species and is one of the five basic elements of nature. Sky is the endless space surrounding the universe. The universal concept of sky as something infinite and eternal is beyond the imagination of human beings.

Some of the main principles of Vaastu are:

The square stands as a symbol of the Vedic view of the cosmos or the universe, and is considered by Hindus to be the shape of the most perfect form, and a perfect reflection of balance and harmony. Its fixed and symmetrical form is that which is present in the celestial realm.

A building is a living organism and can be designed in harmonic resonance with the underlying energy structure of the universe. It becomes a generator of coherence, attuning occupants to universal laws and increasing health, wealth and spiritual well-being.

Right Direction:
The orientation of a building has a dramatic and easily measured impact upon the quality of life of its occupants.

Right Placement of Rooms:
Vedic buildings are designed so that energies from the sun correspond to the specific activities performed within the building.

Right Proportion:
Proportion is a key to successful design in nature. Right proportion in the interior and exterior of buildings can connect individual intelligence to cosmic intelligence

***

Natural, Nontoxic Materials and Solar Energy

Vedic architecture promotes natural and nontoxic construction materials. It also emphasizes filling rooms with sunlight and fresh air, as well as the use of photovoltaics for on-site energy generation.

This may sound a lot like Feng Shui, but there are big philosophical differences. Numerous websites attempt to decipher the differences between the two. Whether or not one subscribes to the Vedic belief system, it is hard to deny that many aspects of these design principles echo current trends for sustainable and eco-friendly building. In addition, Vedic architecture seems to be taking off, possibly for these very reasons.

It has been written that the skyscraper in the state of Maryland called 'Tower II' was designed based entirely on the ancient Vedic mathematics and Natural Law principles. Developer Jeffrey S. Abramson says, "We spend 90 percent of our time indoors, and therefore the built environment has the potential to help a person to succeed. That's why I'm interested in Vedic architecture".

The major factors to keep in mind when you are selecting a lot are:

1. Geographical surroundings,
2. Level of the land,
3. Roads around the plot.
4. Other Basic Principles Of Vaastu Shastra

For people who are planning to buy a plot of land, make sure you get one that is in Southwest, South or West directions. These plots are considered more advantageous than others are. Plots that are square or rectangular in shape are better than irregularly cut ones. Also, the plot should be sloping toward the North & East or Northeast.

At the time of construction of a building, make sure that it has open space on all sides.

The levels of open space should be higher on the South and West sides and lower on the North and East side.

If you construct more than one floor, prepare the first floor on the Southwest. The height of the first floor should not exceed that of the ground floor. Also, make sure that there is no storeroom on the first floor.

Note: The 'center' is the place of *Brahmasthana*. This area should always be left clear. Human activity should be avoided.

The entrance to the house should ideally be in the Northeast, East or North direction. This will bring good luck, prosperity and harmony to the house.

- In case you have a large house with extra rooms, use the room situated in the Northwest direction as a guest room. It is a space that has movement for travelers. If you want your children to move out, this room carries energy encouraging them to do so.

- Since the center denotes Brahmasthan, make sure it is free from any sort of obstruction. There should be no beams, pillars, fixtures, toilet, staircase or even walls in the sacred space.
- As for the shape and size of the door, the width of the door should be half the height of the door.
- Paintings and statues in the house are also an important consideration when it comes to Vaastu Shastra. Pictures depicting war, violence or any negativities of life like sorrow and struggle should not be in the house.
- The living room is best located in the East, North and Northeast directions. According to Vaastu, the main bedroom should be positioned in Southwest, South or West direction of the house.
- The kitchen should be in the *Agni Kond*. Ideally, the best bet is to have the kitchen in the Southeast. In case you cannot have it in the Southeast direction, one in the Northwest or East direction is also considered favorable.
- The study or office should be designed in such a way that you study facing East or North side.

***

Vaastu Directions for the Home

DIRECTION	PLANET	LORDSHIP	BEST LOCATION
Northwest **AIR**	Moon	Vayu (Wind)	Guests, bathroom, garage, animals, utilities, pantry
North Wealth	Mercury	Kubera (Wealth)	Mirrors (North wall), jewels, children, familyroom, basement
Northeast **WATER**	Jupiter	Ishanya (Supreme Lord)	Prayer, spiritual, knowledge, living room, sun porch, patio
West Darkness	Saturn	Varuna (Waters)	Children's room, study, office, den
East Inspiration	Sun	Surya (Health)	Dining room, family room, bay windows, mirrors on East wall,
Southwest **EARTH**	Rahu	Nairuti Dissolution	Heavy objects, bedroom, or bath rooms
South Past Duty Death	Mars	Yama (Lord of Death)	Dining room, no main entrances, bedroom, bathroom
Southeast **FIRE**	Venus	Agni (Lord of Fire)	Kitchen, appliances, computers, exercise room, garage, weights

Blueprints

The Cardinal Directions:
North, West, South, and East
The Intermediate directions:
Northwest, Southwest, Southeast, Northeast and center.

Each of these directions and sub-directions has its own merits and demerits and yields results accordingly.
Every direction has a deity or lord that rules it. (i.e.: spirit energy of wealth)

We learn in our early school years that the earth spins on a North-South axis that tilts to the Northeast.
Positive energy enters through the gateway in the Northeast, and this sector of the home is to remain 'special' and not cluttered.

Vaastu science ...
aligns building design and construction with the principles of cosmic creation and the eternal pulse of

universal life. Such a vibrant structure becomes a living, conscious, breathing entity, capable of interacting intelligently with its human co-creators and co-stewards of planet earth. Everything is alive, connected and changing.

In Chennai, I talked with a pioneer in reviving ancient traditional architecture and he spoke of his concerns in creating such a building. By using Vaastu architecture where all aspects of design and construction are taken into account, this included ... the terrestrial and celestial environments, the individuals involved, and the resonant qualities of all building materials utilized.

- Musical or sound resonance (manifested feeling patterns).
- Mandala or universal energy grid. The direction and impact of energy flows involving terrestrial, biological, and celestial forces; and including the principles of implosion and explosion.
- Light vibrations and color rays on both subtle and physical planes (manifested thought patterns).
- **Form:** cube, pyramid, octagon, circle, and hexagon, the dynamics of multi-dimensional physics. Through geometric form, specific energy qualities and forces are emphasized (manifested light forms and sound form).
- Space-time-measurements involve the inherent values and qualities of numbers, dimensions, frequencies, and time units (Time = Space).
- In traditional Vaastu science, these are applied to human creations through physical measurements defined by *ayaadi* calculations.

Negative Effects in Construction

* Synthetically manufactured materials add further confusion to our modern challenges of life.

* Synthetic plastics and vinyls induce static electrical charges within the indoor environment
* These charges interact with air molecules to produce an imbalanced positive ionization in the oxygen content.
* These synthetically induced phenomena become another potent component in oxygen-related diseases and augment the growing need for oxygen ionizers. Electric ionizers also contribute to imbalanced electrical fields, which, in turn, affect both air quality and the human nervous system.
* **Synthetic plastics** in domestic plumbing are known to change the resonance and vitality of

the water in various ways. Another consideration is that a counter-clockwise rotation induced into the water flow influences its magnetic memory.
- Taken into the body, this water reverses the natural magnetic flow of the cells and may contribute to cell mutation and other unnatural cell development. A clockwise rotation of the flowing water induces the opposite effect: healthy cell growth.
- Steel reinforcement carries and spreads negative electro-magnetic fields in health impacting ways. Steel may also change certain biological geo-electromagnetic fields, creating varying degrees of stress and tension for biological life forms within the indoor environment.
- Compressed wood products containing formaldehyde glues, recycled plastics, synthetic rubber, etc. usually off-gas into the indoor environment, and even seep into the soil when in contact.
- Soil vitality, water quality, and human health are inevitably affected with new and increasing symptoms appearing over time.
- Many of these toxins are the result of accumulated effects, and some may only reveal themselves after two or three generations. Vibrational toxins generate the same effects as biological toxins, often with increased potency.
- Vibrational balancing may be the most basic and potent of all healing tools.
- Some of the more stable synthetic plastic compounds are acceptable for specific

purposes, while the vegetable silica and other biological and non-toxic plastic compounds are ideal for multiple uses.

- In terms of other materials, nowadays marble is highly used in shopping complexes and in residential premises. Research study on selected houses using marble flooring shows that people have a stressful life. The family members were victims of frequent sickness. Use of marble in the bedroom and bathroom is highly inauspicious. This brings poor luck for the occupants.

***

COLOR

Vaastu colors suitable to use when painting your house.

Colors have the capacity of pacifying our mind and stimulating our energy. Our mood, health, happiness are all affected by the colors of our house.

Colors can have emotional, intellectual, materialistic, intuitive and other types of influence on humans.

Red color:
power and ability, is known for its vitality and zest. It displays warmth and enlightens your mood the moment you look at it. Due to the qualities it possesses, red is one of the favored colors to be used at home. Red represents power and valor. It is dramatic in mood, emotional, active and ignites passion and desire. It enlivens the interior space and creates excitement and enthusiasm for life.

However, red should not be used in the bedroom, as it is too energizing. When used in the bedroom, it can be overpowering and stressful for the ones anxious by nature.

Green color:
represents harmony and peacefulness. As green is symbolic of nature, it generates calm and inner peace in the house. Green used in the study room augments intelligence. Since green brings quick healing and rejuvenation as well, disturbed people or those who need refreshment can calm themselves.

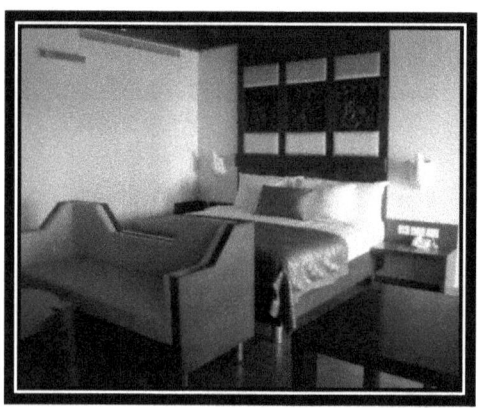

Blue color:
Blue color represents stability, serenity and infinity by symbolizing the cool side of nature and can defuse strong emotions, improving judgment, just like water, it can calm down fire.

Orange color:
has its own beauty, due to its ethereal qualities. The color inspires spirituality as it represents transcendence and an otherworldly aspect of life. This is considered the

best color for your dining room as orange color has the ability to stimulate your appetite.

Communication, positive feelings, cheerfulness and interaction are enhanced in the dining room or living room with orange. Peach color can also be used in the dining hall, as it gives a cool affect.

Pink color:
Pink can be used in the master bedroom or bedrooms located in the South and Southwest direction. It is a color, which reflects joy, happiness and pure feelings, essential for a happy life.

White color
Recommended by Vaastu for your ceilings as white symbolizes purity. It also reflects light and brightens the room. In a bedroom located in the Northwest direction, white can be used.

INDIA, Vaastu Living

Traveling in this country that is about a third the size of Canada (India covers 3.3 million square kilometers and Canada covers 9.9 million square kilometers), I found India to have an impressive population nearing of 1.3 billion people, a dramatic increase over my Canadian population of a mere 35 million people. While India is the second most populous country in the world (after China), Canada has the second largest area in the world (after Russia).

Visiting homes in Mumbai, Delhi or cities in Kerala, I always found that the people regarded their homes as a sacred temple. Hindus remove their shoes before entering the home to make sure the filth of the streets and the world's impurities are kept outside, keeping the interior sacred.

During my visits, I learned that people reveal their high regard for nature by bringing it indoors. Their connectedness to nature was to reflect the rhythm of the universe within their dwelling by bringing plants and natural products (clay pots, jute baskets, sisal rugs, flowers) into their home. All gardeners know that greenery has its own cycle of life, part of this rhythm. Sunlight has its universal rhythm that connects to all life forms and we all react to its changes. Hindus are a culture that likes to face East when they study, read, sleep with their head in the East and even take their bath in the East ~ cleansing.

I could see that nature was also visible in the home with

spices of garlic bulbs and red chilies in view. Displaying a collection of stones, seashells, pinecones, acorns, shelled nuts, baskets and boxes of woven materials all represent earthy textures and products. Nature can also be displayed in the art hung on the walls with landscape scenes or etchings that use earthy tones. Flooring and window treatments can honor nature by using organic materials. Stone, metal and wood are other high-energy materials. It is important to honor the elements and be close to natural products.

Vaastu Shastra prescribes favorable forms or shapes for sites and buildings based on flow of energy. A lot of the rules are attributed in a way that they are in line with the cosmos creation - the sun's path, the rotation of the earth, magnetic field, etc. The morning sun is especially beneficial and purifying, hence the East area is a treasured direction.

The body is considered a magnet with the head, the heaviest and most important part, being considered the North Pole and the feet the South Pole. Sleeping with one's head in the North is said to cause a repulsive force with the earth's magnetic North and thus is harmful. Vaastu architecture starts from site selection, short-listing the raw materials best suited for the construction, directions of the doors, interior designing in sync with the Vaastu Directions and the use of appropriate Vaastu remedies for the prevalent Vaastu Dosha. Vaastu gives you different architectural plans for different buildings depending upon their use.

During my stay in India, a guide Satish directed me to

speak with people working with Vaastu on a daily basis. In the state of Kerala (one of twenty-eight states) it was explained to me by local engineers and architects that throughout history, the type of constructional features illustrates the social class and living standards for generations to come and should stand the test of time and Vaastu Shastra, the building Science, helps in the construction of any type of building.

The book known as *'Thantrasamuchayam'* is used in this state as a guideline for residential construction. This area is known for its mixture of plain and hilly areas with nearly eight months of monsoon rains, thus the shape and construction of buildings have distinct features. They follow the guidelines for construction in terms of numerical measurements - a perfect blend with nature and surroundings and accord a balance with all natural forces.

I studied numerous structures and certain features became obvious, such as the preferable place for the house to be situated is the Northeast or Southwest. The kitchen is also suited to the same location within the building. It is not the appearance, but the calculations that make a 'Vaastu' house.

Property selection:

Property lots facing a North and East Road give overall prosperity.
Property lots facing a West Road give name and fame.
Property lots that are facing a South Road are good for business.
Property lots that are facing East and South Roads are good for females.
Property lots facing West and North Roads are good.
Property lots facing South and West Roads are average.
Properties facing North and South Roads are average.
Properties having roads on three sides are weak lots.
Properties having roads on all sides are the best lots.
Lots facing a road with a T-junction are weak lots.
Lots at the end of a road are not good lots.

***

Mumbai (Bombay)

From the airport, on an intensely hazy day, I headed South into the claw-shaped peninsula occupied by twenty-plus million inhabitants in Mumbai with more than five million housed in slum districts. While crossing the impressive, long Bandra Worli Sea Link bridge, I had an amazing view of modern day construction crowding out pre-war architecture on one side and the Arabian Sea on the other. It is quite misleading to call Mumbai an island today; for it is no longer an island in the full sense of geographical expression; but is a peninsula attached to the mainland. Some historians are of the opinion that all the islands were part of the mainland during prehistoric times and became separated by volcanic action.

Today, Mumbai is known as the most cosmopolitan city in the country, the population comprises of people of Koli, Bhandari, Indo-Aryan, Parsee, Jewish, Muhammadan, Arab, Portuguese, Armenian, English, Scottish, Irish and Welsh origin. Mumbai has developed into India's commercial capital with several leading financial, industrial and commercial centers located in this vibrant city. The people are young. India's median age is 27 years while in Canada the median age is 41 years.

Not far from the Ferry Terminal and the Gateway of India Arch, I chatted with one of the architects working on the hotel where I was staying. We spoke regarding her views for the interior of a home and what she thought carried importance.

"Bedrooms, especially the master bedroom, carry good energy when located in the Southwest, while children's rooms are ideally placed on the West side. For developing better concentration in children, their study area should be separate from but close to their bedroom. For the kitchen, the right location insures the health of the occupants, and Southeast is recommended. Never have a bathroom in the center of the home, or there will be constant mishaps." She explained that offices were recommended to be placed in the North, East or Northeast, attracting positive effects from different planets. Mercury increases brainpower, Jupiter enhances wisdom, Sun raises ambition and Venus instills creativity in new thoughts and ideas.

Traveling in the Northern part of the country brought many ideas and different perspectives.

Taking a lunch break in a small roadside stop not far out of Agra, I chatted with the owner of the establishment. He told me that when building his home, he had a Vaastu rule of thumb he called his own ten 'commandments.'

1st commandment: The main water source of a water feature should be toward the Northeast.
2nd commandment: The kitchen stove should be toward the Southeast.
3rd commandment: The guest room, storage or children's bedroom should be toward the Northwest.
4th commandment: The master bedroom (or a CEO's office) should be toward the Southwest.
5th commandment: The center should be light and airy.
6th commandment: There should be more open space toward the North and East than in the South and West.
7th commandment: The South and West floor levels should be higher than the North and East.
8th commandment: The South and West boundary wall should be higher than the North and East walls.
9th commandment: The entrance should be the North or East.
10th commandment: You should sleep with your head toward the South and raise the headside by three inches.

Rahul, the owner's second son, offered information as to how their lot had been selected.
"Vaastu deals with making the lot ready for construction. We had an ideal lot in square almost rectangular form aligned properly in the four main directions. A compound wall was constructed first. The lot was divided into 81 squares of equal size, and a plan was drawn. Then construction work started after offerings had been made to deities and planets. Vaastu also gives advice on how to match the name of

a person to the place where he wants to live, and how to find the direction for the main entrance into his house. The general placement of rooms in a house is given in the diagram."

***

Basic Construction Considerations:

- Keep open space all around the building.
- Buildings should be constructed higher in the Southwest and lower in the Northeast.
- There should be no tall trees in the East. Trees in the West are good.
- If there is a well or any other pit in the Southeast, Southwest or Northwest direction, there will always be quarrels and mishaps in the family and there will be no peace.
- If an addition is to be constructed, it should extend on all sides. Extending only one side is not auspicious. Newly built houses without Vaastu considerations are believed to carry negative energy, and several troubles or difficulties may arise in the family. Therefore, Vaastu *Poojan* is a must.
- The West portion of the land should be raised. It is auspicious that it slopes towards the East.
- Only new wood is used in construction of a new house. Old, used wood is inauspicious and must be avoided.
- There should not be five corners in the ceiling (irregular shape room).
- There should be no doors or windows on the

Southwest side.
- If there are columns in a building, they should be in even numbers.
- No circular columns in the Northeast corner.
If any columns are exposed for architectural purposes, their number should also be even.
- It is not auspicious to construct anything toward the South or West of the Vaastu zone. Construction should be done toward the North and East of this zone.
- Cactus should not be planted or kept in the house.
- All the doors should open toward the inside so that energy may remain inside. Efforts should be made to leave the rooms open on the Northeast side. Southern or Southwestern portions of a building are ideal for locating staircases.
- Flow of water and its outlet in directions other than East, Northwest, Northeast and North is inauspicious and causes troubles.

***

India Institute of Technology, Delhi

During my travels, there was a great deal of discussion regarding the '**Vaastu pyramid'**. It is believed to play a vital role in astrology, color therapy, self-healing and other para scientific techniques. **Vaastu Shastra** is all about obeying the rules of directions, but since it is not always possible to abide by such strict rules; the pyramid can solve various problems and keep all your harms at bay.

The Greek word 'Pyramid' is a term that is composed of two words - pyra and mid. While '*pyra*' stands for fire, the universal life energy or cosmic force, the word '*mid*' denotes middle or center core. Pyramids have slanting sides meeting at the top, so a pyramid harnesses cosmic energy and preserve it in its bosom. Pyramids that create energy can help in the correction or alteration of Vaastu. They exhibit positive energy and can neutralize the negative energy caused amongst any of the premises due to incorrect Vaastu.

A group of students studying at the university in Varanasi explained that as a unique revolutionary solution, Pyramid Vaastu combines time-tested concepts of ancient wisdom with a new age approach. It balances the electromagnetic field of the human aura (energy field), thereby harmonizing mind, body, spirit and environment. Another major advantage of the pyramid is that it corrects defects without physically altering, shifting or breaking any house, office, shop, factory, sick unit or corporate establishment. As a result, it has been deciphered that pyramids were essentially constructed to harness the cosmic energies.

They are a new concept of energy-corrections that achieve all these things in a hassle-free manner. The common link between Vaastu Shastra and Pyramid Vaastu is channeling cosmic energies for constructive purpose. While Vaastu Shastra was conceived for the betterment of mankind, pyramids were constructed for the benefit of the Pharaohs and their souls, reflecting negative energies. It represents many aspects regarding positive energy for its surroundings as the triangle shape is also the representation of fire-energy, which can heal as well as destroy.

As I contemplated these things, wherever I looked I noticed some form of the pyramid that has brought about a revolution in the field of Vaastu Shastra. From the American one dollar bill, to tops of financial institutions, malls, skyscrapers, and condominiums, we find the pyramid used as a correction for negative energy flow. It is used just as a candle is lit to cleanse a room of negativism.

The power is in the multiplier 9 x 9 calculations. The pyramid shape itself attracts geological, biological, cosmic energy-particles from around the environment. Pyramids are strange creations and their wonderful miraculous power of healing is a surprise even to scientists.

The pyramid and its conception has puzzled and attracted the attention of people for many centuries. Its history, shape and size have been a mystery for many eras. Pyramids are used to correct the Vaastu defects of a particular place or room. They are known to remove blocks.

Today, many individuals consume Pyramid water as a healthy tonic. Food kept in/under the pyramid is tastier and known to remove the bad effects of food. For success, good health and protector of negative energy, the pyramid survives in several different aspects.   **2010 Olympic Flame – Vancouver**

The Adage 'health is wealth'.

This holds a lot of meaning in Vaastu Shastra for keeping in good health and remaining in the best of spirits.

- It is evident in India that temple architecture is based on pyramidal shapes. The design, which also incorporates domes, places the main idol under a pyramid-shaped roof to generate energy among devotees. This is why people visiting Hindu temples with such roofs come away feeling cleansed and energetic.
- A house should be designed in such a way so that there is maximum entry of sunlight and proper cross-ventilation.
- Vaastu defects refer to any obstacle in the way of cosmic energy flow in a building, which could adversely affect and disturb the cosmic energy field levels or the bio-energy flow fields and force. Such an obstacle creates an uncomfortable environment for people staying in the building, and this "disharmony" of cosmic and bio-energy forces may be called a Vaastu defect. Demolition may be the correction needed.
- According to Vaastu Shastra, a staircase in the exact center of a house would lead to health problems. So, take care to get the stairs built in a corner.
- Make sure that there are no overhead beams running through the center of a house or they could lead to a disturbed mind.
- The *Brahmasthan* should be kept open and free from heavy objects, pillars and beams. Install a

Reiki charged crystal grid in the Brahmasthan, to keep the whole house energized.

- One of the main causes behind sickness is an imbalance of the fire element in the house. If your house faces South, with a slope toward that direction, the possibility of health problems will continue to exist. To cure the situation, make sure that the gate along the South wall always remains shut. The gate should be made of wood and be high enough that the road outside is not visible.
- Lighting a candle daily in the fire zone (Southeast direction) is important for good health.
- Vaastu links health and illness with the placement of the kitchen in a house. If the kitchen is not located in the fire zone, the occupants will be vulnerable to health disorders. So, always plan the kitchen in the Southeast direction.
- The boundary wall of the house should be of the same height as the gate. Growing plants on both sides of the gate promotes good health.
- If someone is ill, keep a burning candle in his/her room for a couple of weeks.

Bedrooms

General health improves by sleeping with the head toward the South. Sleeping on the left is recommended for people with "*Vaatha*" and "*Khapha*" constitutions, while sleeping on the right is recommended for those with "*Pittha*" constitutions.

- Never put a mirror in front of the bed. Cover mirrors while sleeping to avoid bad dreams. The

bed should never touch the wall. Leave a hand-space between the two.
- Avoid or minimize the use of T.V. or computer in a bedroom, as the energy level of the room will be destroyed by the radiation emitted.
- Never sit or sleep under an overhead beam to avoid depression, headache or loss of memory. Pregnant women should never sleep in a Northeast room to avoid risks of miscarriage or abortion.
- Open a North and Eastern window rather than a Southwestern window to promote health, happiness and harmony in the family.
- Metal beds (wrought Iron) are not recommended, because of health problems related to the heart and brain.
- Fluorescent tubes can interfere with vibrations of the body, causing people to be hyperactive and irritable.

Negative energy

This comes from heavy objects, waste or a shoe rack found in Northeast and North of your house. That area should be kept clean and light. Heaviness there will block financial growth.

Do not face south while cooking, or your mind will be filled with negative thoughts.

***

India,
the Mother of Vaastu

Remya was a 23 year old woman whom I met in Kochi on the way to Kovalam. I met her when our bus driver and tour guide decided it would be a good idea for us to experience and attend a Hindu wedding. Uninvited, nineteen of us dressed in typical traveling tourist apparel marched into the hall as the ceremony was about to begin and found ourselves whatever seats were available. Remya and Shibu were fulfilling their final vows. This amazing, welcoming crowd of over a thousand attendees smiled at our group of Canadians as they viewed our unexpected visit as prosperous, bringing positive energy to the wedded couple from thousands of miles away. It was regarded as their destiny, good fortune and added new luck.

I was privileged to have a young, well-spoken Indian native next to me who explained in detail all the Hindu ceremonial meanings and procedures. They invited our group to their celebration lunch afterwards, but we had to decline so as not to delay our arrival at the next destination. I did have time for a lengthy conversation with the group sitting next to me where I enquired about the youth of the country and their point of view of the ancient Vaastu study.

Arvind had travelled to more than twenty of India's twenty-eight states. He explained: *'There is a Vaastu following now worldwide. Science has proven that the positive effects of a proper Eastern orientation on the brain and behavior are now being documented by modern science and recent EEG research points to greater efficiency of neuronal functioning when our head is oriented towards the East, rather than the North. Anyone can feel the vibes of a place are not right when they enter a building. You can actually feel better shopping or working in one place over another.'* He hesitated for a moment, and then continued. *'You talk about Feng Shui that regards south as a fame and recognition area whereas Indian science considers it inauspicious. The sun plays a major importance in the design and allocation of rooms.'*

Aryind's brother commented that the quantum physicist, John Hagelin, from Harvard advised G.W. Bush to close the South entrance of the White House, as this would help him make wiser and more intelligent decisions. He headed an organization called US Peace Government.

Indians believe that the science of Vaastu, according to their sacred principles, was designed to attract nature's auspicious influences and block inauspicious ones.

During our conversation, which attracted other Hindu people from the congregation, the subject of their great Indian temples came up. *'Our temples have been in existence for centuries and are a standing testimony to the profundity of this science. They are enclosed within a compound wall, keeping more space toward the Northeast corner of the building, which is left open with more windows to allow entry of the auspicious rays of the morning sun. The main gate is kept clear of obstructions like trees, rocks or excessive foliage that may block the flow of positive energy from entering.'*

Niranja was a dancer with the Kathakali dance theatre, the Indian ancient storytelling troupe. She explained. *'Though all the directions are good and auspicious by the grace of the supreme God, self-satisfaction and spiritual peace is obtained from prayers offered in the Northeast direction. Northeast direction is very important in the construction of a building. No large and heavy rooms or materials should be kept in this portion. The owners cannot progress if they violate this rule, nor can they develop and flourish. It is written that if this portion is extended outwards and open, it provides all happiness.'*

The small gathering moved along with me as I followed the crowd to the outside of the hall. Several hundred other guests went to another location for their meal and celebrations. A woman draped in elaborate turquoise silks, wearing frameless lenses, listened quietly, but I noticed she worked her way closer to me. I was anxious to hear what she had to say. I introduced others and myself from our group. A woman doctor, Tara, spoke in a soft tone in perfect English, perhaps educated in the West.

'Did you know that there are four types of Vaastu?' she began. 'Firstly Bhoomi - deals with selection of a site/land. Secondly, Prasada - deals with buildings. Thirdly, deals with transportation of vehicles, carts and ships and fourthly, Sayana – deals with furniture, tools and utensils. It is good if a building is aligned strictly in the four main directions because its walls will be either perpendicular or parallel to the magnetic lines of earth. If we build a house putting an entrance in any of the four main directions, there will be prosperity for the resident. But if the house is oriented into the corner directions, then the walls cross the magnetic lines in a zigzag way, leading to mental disturbances and lack of peace and success.'

Interesting, I thought. I asked about health issues and what were her thoughts regarding the bedroom.

'The bedroom is a place where one can be totally oneself. It is the room where we spend most of the time to sleep and relax. I recommend that lighting should be a soothing general illumination. Lights should be planned in such a way to create a romantic, relaxing environment. Table lamps or hanging lampshades provide the room with a very esthetic look. One should never sleep under a beam, as this will affect one's *health. The placement of the bed is important just as the mystical nature of directions, cosmology and the larger quest of people for their spiritual awakening can be addressed through the design. I like to think of it as a medical science.'*

We sat next to one another near the gates of the property as I waited for the call to return o the bus. Tara continued as others asked questions. '*Just like Vaastu, the origins of Ayurveda, a health system, originated in ancient India and share a common goal. The house creates a barrier between man and the elements and must be constructed a certain way so not to become an obstruction. Ayurveda is a system of balance, living in accordance with nature's laws. If the mind is upset, the whole body is thrown out of balance, inducing illness.'*

Across the roadway, I noticed some of our group nearing the bus. Tara's daughter, a Computer Science student jumped into the conversation when I asked about their thoughts on Vaastu pyramid study. She explained. '*A few years ago, the dead body of an Egyptian princess Mene, was examined. It had been kept for thousands of years in a pyramid. The examination showed to our great surprise that her skin cells were still functioning although she had been dead nearly 3000 years. Isn't it miraculous?'*

Tara concluded with… '*Scientists thought that mummification prevented decay of the dead body cells of the mummies that had been kept within Pyramid Space. The pyramids usefulness for curing social, psychological, domestic and physical problems was a simple and cheap treatment of several diseases. It has been recorded that pyramids create co-ordination in life by removing inter-personal conflicts and turns out the negative powers from your house and helps to circulate peace that leads to a happy and prosperous life.'*

Now it was my time to gather my thoughts and head back to the bus with the literature given to me by the twelve-year-old daughter of the groom's aunt. The vibrant colorful dress of the many guests flashed before my eyes as the bus pulled onto the dusty roadway and headed to my next destination. India, a place of extreme contrasts.

***

Why is the world interested in ancient studies?

The purpose of ancient China and India studies was to identify instability and create a calm, healthy, harmonious environment for your well-being where the mind, body and spirit become balanced with universal energy.

The world today, as we see it through electronic devices and no longer newspapers, is bursting with new inventions on a daily basis. The materialistic ways of the West are becoming common everywhere and turning lifestyles into a state of chaos. People are searching for a sense of calm, a peacefulness that will ward off rare illnesses and diseases. The daily chatter of an active mind now dominates every minute of every hour. Times of rest and self-relaxation are few and far between, with no energy left for contemplation.

The time once spent listening to nature is almost non-existent. There is no time to focus on the meditation of following the inhale and exhale of our own breath with sudden stops for enlightenment, which the sages did to obtain their wisdom. The study of Patanjali aphorisms is almost non-existent compared to a few centuries ago. Ironically, the West is seeking insight from the East, while the East is turning to materialism.

The spread of ancient studies for harmony and balance is taken very seriously by architects and designers around the world. They wish to create healthy buildings and a renewed lifestyle free of multi-tasking. Stress caused by an overactive mind is lacking a harmonious environment. Outside space must be calm so that the body can rest and absorb the healing flow of the cosmic energies. Harmony with nature both inside and outside ourselves can be attained by learning to have what we need and nothing more. Greed is the ego of desire. Let go and be cleansed. The ancients said the less you had, the less you had to worry about, so that you could fill yourself with knowledge, wisdom and harmonious energies while in a relaxing atmosphere.

These practices offer ways and means to focus on yourself. By reducing your activities, you have time to learn how you 'feel' about things, places and people. Take some quality time and focus on yourself. Notice how you react to certain people, colors, shapes, places, foods, and other items. Ask yourself if you like them or not. Would you change them if you could? It is about the need for a calm, uncluttered space to quiet the mind and talk back to the constant chatter of intrusions. Tell them to 'Take a hike!' It's quiet time!

Creating a home for the soul, your true self is the goal of these ancient studies. Live right, eat right – naturally. Good light, fresh air, natural foods and healthy materials in your buildings, clothes and vehicles will all add up to a longer, more purposeful life minus the chemical off-gassing substances.

Keep things simple and remember that everything in moderation is good. Once a week is better than once a day. Listen to music that feeds the soul, which will heal the body just as laughter has been known to do. Energy flow from the eight directions surrounds us no matter where we stand on the planet. Some directions are healthier than others are, as we all have different needs. Start mapping your own needs, giving yourself time everyday to heal. Attract positive energy by making your own corrections in favor of a more harmonious lifestyle with less 'chatter' in your mind. Pay attention to where you are happiest and to the surrounding colors, shapes and materials.

Since these ancient studies need to know where you are happiest, so they can truly reflect your personality and be aligned to your personal needs, be honest and list your needs. Remember the ayurveda rule, *like increases like*. For example... if you have a *vata* (air) constitution and you find your memory is not just poor but declining, you could be spending too much time in the Northwest realm, which belongs to the element air. If you are sleeping or working in this area, like increases like and leads to excess air-energy in the body. This interferes with your well-being.

Take a closer look at each space in your home or workspace. Does each area identify itself and speak to you by reflecting your personality? Or are you (so to speak) not in the picture? Is something amiss? You can read all the books you want, follow all the suggestions and make all the alterations, but if your home doesn't 'feel' just right, then your health will suffer.

The mystical movement of energy is something we

cannot see, but it has the most profound effect on the body as well as the home. Make your own personal list of your favorite... colors, shapes and products. You will soon learn if you are more comfortable living with wood floors or tile, white walls or green walls, floral fabrics or stripes, round or rectangle windows, etc. Make yourself a personal portfolio and collect pictures of what you find pleasing and would be comfortable living with, then try and duplicate your 'likes'. Get rid of things 'you' are not comfortable living with.

Over the years, we all change our opinions, needs and favorite items. Just as the weather changes from season to season, nothing ever stays the same forever. Pay attention to your health. It can tell you when it is time to refresh or change your surroundings. A change will alter the flow of energy within your space thereby aiding in preserving a healthy body.

ANCIENT SECRETS

Every 'thing' vibrates and carries energy.
However, a house carries energy from the land, the architect, the builder and everyone who worked on it, lives in it and everything inside it.
Beware of negative energies that linger.

Author
Mallory Neeve Wilkins
Feng Shui Interior Designer

Fun Schway Journal
Fun Schway Interiors North American Feng Shui
House of the Caduceus (feng shui novel)

Graveyard Autos (photography)
The Laundry Art Book (photography)
Hot-Walker Life on the Fast Track (novel)

www.ingramcontent.com/pod-product-compliance
Lightning Source LLC
Chambersburg PA
CBHW050650160426
43194CB00010B/1879